Of Times Three

Of Times Three
D.B. Smith

This volume is dedicated to my wife, Gayle, an extremely talented and dedicated partner in the art of living.

✣ ✣ ✣

CONTENTS

❈❈❈
Of Nature

Up The Road To Grandeur

Vista beauty spread out beyond a rising offshoot with view
parking,
Overlook, expansive with contrasting colors
Up a narrow, gravel road, winding and steep,
Clean and virtuous, high and deep—
Mystical eye-catcher with changing sky
Answers to anyone's exclaimed "why!"

Contrast in visuals. Solid rock. Solid ground.
Silence and grandeur.
Distant pastels and grandeur.
A shutter's blend of emotion.

God Is Coming

Up the winding road, branching wildly,
Teasing the earth's vegetation, is a spot of fire.
Soughing settles it into slow spreading uncontrolled.
"Wake up, wake up! God is coming"—
If the line from "Out of Africa" is conjured
In startled minds
Dumbfounded by thick smoke and flame.

Pine needles, not coffee, burn.
Underbrush goes up in turn.
Houses to ashes—when will they ever learn?

Sweat and tears and hidden fears
Accompany fevered action.
God's coming has people humming.
Ears pick up the "wheres" of shelters.
Driving home meets barricade.
What the hell's going on?
I'm afraid!
Will nothing but memories stand
When "God is coming" flame is fanned?

It's a blessed shame. And God is to blame.
And God's coming transpires in
Towering spires,
Inspires the use of God's name.

All Came Tumbling Down

Majestic Rock Face, you lie broken.
You stood unmoved many years.
You were unearthed, an ode to a road.
Scenic, you were seen from afar.
Un-mourned, you are rubble.
Blown apart, you are rubble.

When you tumbled down,
Two dreams vanished.
Smashed vehicle—
Death mourned—
Stories—
Road opened—

Majestic Rock Face, you have changed.
Are you passive, neutered, massive but
safe?
Majestic Rock Face, you stood for many
years.
Again you lie broken.
Dreams are unbroken this time.

Ode To Wilderness

Sing an ode to wilderness, to joy, to
uplifting expansiveness.
Wing like high flight that looks down for
sustenance.
Sing unto great loftiness, majesty, spiritual
renewal.
Passionately cry out, "ah, wilderness!'

Be thou the voice of God.
Stretch as wilderness stretches.
Sing white; sing cold; sing of greens,
yellows, reds.
Talk in well modulated voices of great
immodest choices.
Chant of insignificant man
Compared to unspoiled creation.
Fashion emotion that loves wilderness!
Can you be a prayer?

I Am The Poster On The Wall

I am the poster on the wall
In rain hat and slicker and backpack.
I am you who would dislodge time and space;
Discard time, renew space;
Change what seems to what is,
Beyond each new horizon.

I am the traveler you
With pipe and peace of mind and pack.
The turbulent sky you see will pass
Into green grass, trees, rocks, shadows, sun, hills,
weeds,
Green pastures, flowers—new and old.

Take my spirit off the wall.
Be bold!
Say, "Time, I too shall bid the mountains and the
hills goodbye,
God speed!".

Grey Lady Dawn

She comes up with mysterious cat's feet,
Cold at wakefulness, when sunlight is yet a
faint glimmer.
Her inattention is not a rebuff, but a prism
for a shimmer
In something furious torn from the black
page of night.

When the donkey brays in the wrong key,
And the rooster crows at the dim lights
close,
A pale moon begins to fade away.
Grey lady, Dawn, disappears into bright
sun.
All-gone has a light nostalgia to it.

The Moment Of Yes

"Where ya goin, Pilgrim?"
"Out there beyond the pale
Where monsters of the deep dwell."

Story—belief—yes

"How do ya dare, Pilgrim?"
"It's in God's hands. I must go and see."

Many moments of the story of "yes" occupy
the pages of time—
Even into that great ocean of nothing called
space.

Gorgeous Deep

The brightly colored wrigglers drift in slow
motion
Far below the turbulent surface.Varicolored
stars pose for Oceanographers.
Yellow, white, red, paint the "down there"
seascape
Hiding predators..

Perspective

Ever so far away, the spyglass has it first,
from aloft.
Land Ho!
The nearest projection that does not waver
into mirage
Treats perspective as an ally
To surprise its own speck on the horizon.

Sands Of Time

Deserts left as sands of time
Are viewed from a thousand miles or so
As grains of wondrous romance,
Calling upon a long endurance to survive
In human terms that reaffirm the camel's
usefulness.

Sands of beaches provide prosperity as time
rolls on
And the tide's wake is plentiful;
And builders build and bathers bathe
And, barefoot, wonder as they wander
In heat and wavy laps, and ponder.

Sand is in the concrete and leaves an
imprint indiscrete
That all is commercialized and replete with
vacuum.

The sands of time are ever with us
In one form or another.
They lay around without a fuss
In one form or another
And overcome the wounds of crime
That hearts and minds might smother.

The sands of time were.
The sands of time are.
The sands of time will be....
The sands of time.

Bird

Black, screek, ebony slow flight,
Winged low to perch and tweek a branch,
To act absurdly awkward—
A cry to sky is sent squawkward.

Cock an eye toward vivisection
In a worm-squirm connection
That spells a feasting frenzy
In the back yard of Greg McKensey.

Bye-bye, Blackbird,
Fly away home,
Or to Mckensey's neighbor's tree,
Then down to earth for pickings free.

Drinking Song

I've walked a while
And sung my drinking song,
Drinking in the whole outdoors
Without regard to what is wrong.
I belong to the grass carpet floors.
They fit my style.

I've gawked awhile
At ducks and geese and water,
Blinking in the noonday sun
Upon the earth, a giant blotter,
 whose rays are spun
Around a walker's mile.

Equatorial

Neither north nor south, and both,
The equatorial speaks volumes,
As in loud and dinlike.
Unrestricted aviary, airy, detonates explosions
That rock the atmosphere when birds are frightened.

Emotions are heightened where those that mimic man
Yabba and ooh ooh as fruit is devoured.
All the territorial that make up the equatorial
Are showered, then are flowered, in abundance.
The bird is of paradise.
The flowering is of Bird of Paradise.
A great menagerie is of the wild
Where kill and feast abides in humid lushness.

The lion's sartorial is manely.
The zebra has tailored stripes.
Gazelleabrate a sleek attire that allows for speed.
Big cats are bedecked in similar fashion,
As in chase they dash on.
Nature is often cloaked in mist and verdant smells.
And, wonderfully, everything gels.

The human element burns as with fire
And wears little in the way of clothes.
And why these things are this way
Only God in Heaven knows.

Farm Squares

From a window seat
At thirty thousand feet
I gaze at maize,
Wheat, grass, in squares.

I ride aloft on silver wings
And laugh at how absurdly
Nature swings
To the music of the sphere.

The plane's a humming thing.
.The trip's a calming thing,
In looking down belowing,
Watching green things growing.

While up where I am noting
The weather clouding, winding, rocking,
All the crowd is swaying
To the tune of raindrops playing.

Sun and sunlight reappearing
Display in brightness
Farm squares in the clearing.
Is that dot a yearling?

The tricks of shadows
Meet my stares
Until suddenly—
I'm out of squares.

Criss-Cross

Long strings of white clouds
Diffuse across a wide open sky.
They cross each other in flowered patterns
Like paint lines gone awry.
Though jet planes long are gone from sight,
Their contrails are slow to die.

Bougainvillea For Show

Red bracts of bougainvillea gain showy attention,
Flashing about on showy tendrils of vine.
They take over the doorway of the greenhouse
And overshadow flats and pots and potted flowers
And everything earthbound for take-home.
If you grow for gardeners, they will come.
And, "Oh, what a pretty whatzis" tells the story.

Flashion Show

Un-uniform, un-clashing, petunias on parade,
Spilling out of their plot, to out-do any forget-me-not,
Co-mix doubly bright with singular might,
And spell the summer's dazzle with their own alphabet.
Ruffles and flourishes dominate.
Crowding to show many faces, they vie for attention—
Blue ribbon or honorable mention—
Until fresh frost freezes all flowers.

Indecision

They are cute buggers until they grow up.
Green raggedy weeds with prickly leaves
Take hold with roots that shoot straight to hell.
Unchecked, they appear, appear, appear, appear—
Their march through Georgia daunting.
A bushel for the landfill is only a reprieve
From what errant Nature has up her sleeve.
Defoliation may be a solution.
But, God, how I would miss everything not weed!

Desert Air

Flowers gone beyond him who would avoid the sand
Cannot waft a scent,
Cannot brighten a vase,
Cannot heighten a sense of wonder,
Cannot give him pause.

Spots of white, red, yellow, lavender—
Color unseen,
Wasted,
Untested by the eye,
Unimagined,
Are and are not.

A pot could hold a cactus in bloom.

Splendid in the Grass

Itsy bitsy spider says, "It is time to spin a web."
Something silken, shiny, takes shape in the grass.
Patiently, Itsy bitsy weaves finely its silver,
Something in Webdom first class.
Time will pass.
And, so, too, will something tasty,
To be devoured with no motion that is hasty.

Red, Single Bloom

Scarlet top!
It stood out from all other green
Because it bloomed.
It alone fulfilled its mission of;
"Oh! Isn't it pretty?"

Deeply Green

The green, green grass of cloudy
Is pleasing to the eye.
No streaming light will wash away deep green
Before and after rain,
When clouds prevail.

A satisfying richness of contentment overlays,
When grays pervade the days with filtered light
And lawn is dressed in blue-green to tease unfettered sight.

No Match For Evergreen

Small color is no match for overgrown evergreen.
Made miniscule and insignificant,
The dinky daisy is easily overlooked.
The virulent scrub, unattended, is overlooked for occupancy.
Slash tall tulips instead,
Iris for the discerning eye,
Long canes of roses, red.

See how tall green, conical trees stand.
They command attention
Until reds and whites prevail
And hold their own convention before mini sleep,
No match then for ever-green.

The Weather Is Whimsical

Talk to the weather.
You will find it is whimsical.
Now is the hour of peaceful co-existence.
Then is the hour of punishment
By arbitrary elements.
Another hour finds itself being wooed
Unto a great outdoors.

Eye on the weather brings
High wind alert.
Eye on the weather rings out with alarm.
Eye on the weather coos with gentleness.
Eye on the weather news
Gets it all wrong.

It is there in the mind,
Gods pulling the strings.
Talk to the weather.
Perhaps they will listen.

"Hear oh mighty ones
Who from the beginning
Have shared the seasons.
We beat drums, calling for rain.
Transfix for us perfect weather."

Snow Blossoms

A morning's cold
And overnight snow
Help to show off new blossoms,
Coating twiggy sticks,
All rooted in the ground—
Forming "white bush".

Two Faces Of Winter

Look out the window at snow falling;
Warmly look out the window.
Look at the driveway filling—
Gives you a chill.
Smile at the stew pot bubbling.
Look at what's in the stew!
Look out the window at kids playing.
Hear the scream of a fall.
Look out the window at snow falling;
Decide not to drive to the mall.
Snow today gone tomorrow—
Beg, steal, or borrow from Spring.

Sea Boats and Gales

Sea boats and gales, sail boats and rain,
Challenge the heart with pounding refrain.
Point A to point B is never easy,
As far as those on the seas see.

Nature in games of pitch and toss
Will never count the loss,
If gale swept wind and rain at sea
Should overcome the one called me.
Whatever powers my little sea boat
Should keep me upright and afloat;
But though my wish is to travel far,
I'd rather not be windswept to where
I have to cross the bar.

My rudder genuflection
Observes, upon reflection,
That it had better not fail me
In a wind designed to re-gale me.

Becalmed is one thing; another is maelstrom.
{By the looks of things, I may have to bail some.}

I'm turning around, heading for shore.
Trimming my craft is too much of a chore.
My sea boat is too much of a wee boat
To continue, even with a pea coat.
Sea boats and gales?
The storm prevails.

All Is Calm

Ocean, placid, barely rippled shoreline full of bathers.
The sea is calm tonight.
Calm lingers into day, night, day.
Peace upon the waters gives tranquility its name.
Trident, lazyloo, floats indifferently upon the dark blue
depth of happiness.
All is bright before the storm.

Aftermath

The sea is calm tonight.
Runaway mammoth waves,
Subsided, are all quiet.
Flotilla, flotsam, dead,
Devoid-of-reason,
Mix of destruction,
Clash with human existence.
And ride into tolls is misery.
Bleak to the human eye,
Consuming to emotion,
The ocean rolls out and in again.
New possibilities can be measured.

Survivor's Lament

Home! Old times there are not forgotten.
Everything is gone!—
Except the listening post for remembering.
"Let us gather together to pray.
Let us take our tears to the Lord.
Cry for what shall be nevermore.
Cry over the whirlwind's sword.
Knees, dear people.
Be thankful for new life
While remembering the old, destroyed.
"Arise and go forth, dear people, survivors.
Bury your dead with your lamentations.
Take with you a remembrance rock and be
comforted."

Light Show

Well, fry my hide! No, forget that! Don't fall overboard!
Off in the distance, flickering neon lights up the ocean.
Darkness of shadow, overhead, is pierced by jagged storm
javelins.
Black dominates blue. Loud timpani dies off.
It comes around again to the tune of flash, flash, flash!
Sails are ghostly—seen, unseen, seen, lashed to spars,
masts, jibs and booms.
Sail on, sail on, sail on.

After Wowers

Holy Toledo! Good golly, Miss Molly!
Oh look at the pretty whatsis!
Shit and shinola, a shooting star!
Raggedy-ass lightening strike!
Brillig and slithy toves!
Taste the sweet, tart blueberry tart!
Clashing cymbals!
Revisit the mushroom cloud!
Child's-play cacophony!
Vista whew!
Oh, my God!

Cutting Back

Wellsprings bubble up in strength
That spreads the water widely.
In slow times wellsprings weakly go;
And waters recede and slow.
Surprisingly, life as culled and pruned
Goes on anew.

Nature has its own agenda,
Provides its own addenda.
And wellsprings, well again,
Well again,
To take the seeds (including man's)
To fruitfulness in numbers.
Again the blade of drought appears
And swaths away the waters,
And sweeps a path to oblivion for
The sitters on teeter totters.
Ages tweak themselves toward greatness
And back again.

Reflections on the ways of waterways
Reminds the mystery buff
That cutting back is wholesome stuff,
Though recycling life enough
Is never for the faint of heart
In Nature's weakened phase.
The joy of mankind has value
And makes it all worthwhile,
When standing in lushness deep
They see eternal ripeness live,
And begin to smile.
There is method in Nature's style.

Run, River, Run

Shallow and wide, narrow and deep,
A wild ride through the countryside,
Run, river, run.
Fast and slow with great range,
Flow toward the banks to make change.
Run, river, run.
Rocks and foam wherever you roam,
Pressure your waters toward home.
Run, river, run.

Run, River, Run II

Innocent:
The mountain stream just is; and its deep cuts defy measure.
It has no malevolent scheme to undo what has been wrought.
It can only do endlessly what naturally follows from naught
But the pull of gravity, uncovering things one can treasure.
It cannot be maligned, in flowing, as a downhill wanderer.
It has never been taught to create havoc or torture what lives;
Though mishap called accident does occur, something that gives
Vent to one's emotion, gives one reason to deeply ponder.
The mountain stream just is, without need to justify its being.
It can spibble over stones as it drops white, with a leeeky sound.
It can go wide and move silently. It can curve and snake, wound
 In on itself before falling precipitously, with landscape agreeing.
Asking it to do other than what it does, as it wanders and
descends,
Presupposes that different colored roses choose what they will
be.
 Cascade, ripple, slowing, rapids, tracing itself, chasing, racing
free,
This long, progressing water, wearing, channeling,trickling,
bends.

Ruined

Tromp heel art from children's boots
Makes deep footprints in crystalline snow.
The pure drift meets its grand ruin
And tattles on cold feet with red glow
And melts puddles into recesses
In the warm afternoon.

Miss Annie's Palette

Visitors from far and near in the city of Applegate
Took to the streets; they couldn't wait.
Now was planting time from Annie's garden.
She would greet them with smiles while begging their pardon
For walks overgrown with flowers, strewn with debris.
She would walk them through what colors to use,
How to mix colors, fix garden mistakes,
What to plant en-mass or in twos.
Annie gave samples, sometimes bouquets.
She knew all about planting what on what days.

Rose

The rose grows
And is trimmed.
It beautifies its spot of earth.
We could all learn something from the rose
Worth remembering.

Pretender

A brown leaf in freefall
Alights upon a broad leaf
Green upon a flowering weed
And stays, as if it grew
Right there then bloomed.

Green And Gold Symmetry

Two trees stand in a parking lot
One symmetrical in gold
Set against symmetrical in green.
Outlined in green, it stands sympathetically bold.
Both ornamental to the eye,
When straight on they are seen,
Only, the gold will fall away
From the tree that appears to die.

Monarch Moment

Momentarily, a Monarch Butterfly of miniature magnitude
Dove aflutter
And danced out of sight.
Black and orange on warmed air, in grand flight,
Kept apace a shadow doing equal dance
And equaled, I am sure, its counterpart in France.

Sodak Revisited

The Cemented Long Ago

They are, I guess,
As realistic as any sculpture can be
As a bridge to the long ago.
Cemented in our time,
The look-a-likes fleshing out
Excavated bones of what was living in our long ago
Deserve extended stares
From movers through South Dakota.
To some extent they "drive" our cars today.
(The dangers of extinction can leave the fittest unconcerned,
Not recording history,
Completely unaware of God and man.)

Long Division

A length of cowboy country
Wends its way through middle South Dakota.
I have seen the barren side of a long divide
Down through and west of Pierre.
Farm country goes north and south of east of where
The wilderness is spare.

Badger Country

He was tall and wore a goatee.
He told stories in uniform and wrote poetry.
South Dakota Poet Laureate—
The state was Badger country for Charles Badger Clark.
Poet in Residence at Dakota Wesleyan—
One year when I was there.
He pointed with disdain to the campus hodge-podge architecture.
I attended Hot Springs High School ('49 to '53).

Prairie

Slammed up against the highest hills
When the black mountains were new,
Flat, dry, spare corn country
Stretches from town to town with view
And dribbles into cattle ranches, sage, and blue.

The "dare you to survive" country
Has Badlands, jack-a-lopes (not), arroyos, gorges,
 A wild look, skeletal remains, rattle snakes
And dry river beds with rot.

How can one not love its border spots
Where sunflowers grow?
Where prairie winds and tumbleweeds blow?
Dakota Wesleyan took note long ago.

Scarlet In Glorious Defeat

I watched the twilight
Do magic with the sky.
The paint box spilled
The various shades of grey of clouds;
And brilliant edges formed
As red ran off toward west
And faded into that lavender
The lessening light enhanced.
Suddenly black proclaimed a victory.
I mourned the passing of the sun,
As it declaimed its valedictory.

Slips Of Lavender

Oops! The red has gone lavender
In early morning grey.
Slips of lavender greet a new day, dawning.
Light behind a strip of redness
Gathers in intensity;
And a voice inside me stresses,
"Let it be! Let it be!
But, not the voice of deep regret,
Nor song of deep remorse,
Nor song of fading darkness
When lavender slips away.

✽✽✽
OF ART

Birth, A Necessary End

Art rejoices to be free from quarantine.
Uneven breaks the dawn of a new creation
And, time is needed to bring elation
Around to reason.
Inhibited mastermind in scenes of chaos,
Protected until now carpenter of paradise,
Can produce nothing.

A twisted string causes pain to the puppet
Who, in anguish, doubts invested power
With which in some protracted hour
Yet undecided,
He has to listen to a muse,
Confuse the devil, doubt,
And choose to confront us with an ark
Of magnitude and merit.

Can he bear it?
Yes, for only in a brief and candid span
Did Keats perform upon the earth.
Yet, genius guided and confided
Long enough that he was able
To confront us with a fable concerning beauty.
Resolute and forsaking, giving up for good the road not taken,
Emerges Artist in ernest dedication.
Blasting out indelicately the form and features,
He obeys the formidable teachers,
But adds to them a veritable barrage
Of line, distortion, trial, evasion,
Modeled emotions not used 'till now.
Modified to fit the framework of life's window,
His masterpiece, cast at last,
Increases and comes forth!

Little Venus

A starkly poignant photograph
Graphically displays a little Venus, naked,
Running from Hell.
A quiet unassuming life shattered in consequence of war
Talks more, much more, than a thousand words
Of unintended threat to all that mattered to her.

And war shall have its dominion,
In spite of heartfelt opinion.
(Repeat chorus)

There was nothing personal in the act or in capturing its consequence.

Little Venus did not win the prize.
She was only the object of composition and focus.
Little Venus had all that could be said in her eyes.

War will have its dominion
In spite of heartfelt opinion.
(Repeat chorus)

All the world's a stage on which to act out rage
On a scale difficult to gauge,
War dispassionately to wage.
Little Venus could not fly and was trapped.
Yet, her flight was old fashioned naked truth, captured,
An indictment of the low road to war.
One can only say with Sandburg, all were "surprised by what happened." [1]
If anything is unpredictable, it is war.

War will have its dominion
In spite of heartfelt opinion.

---

[1] "The Unknown War", Carl Sandburg

Still Life Blank

Old woman, why do you stare?
Do visions of a brighter future
Still flash before unblinking eyes?
Has Depression depression redesigned them
To reflect a national capsize?
There you are on the stoop resigned
To day after day the same,
No hope, no will, no wonder apparent, nothing otherwise.

As still-life, you are forever, old woman.
In life you precede a slow upward endeavor.
Can you ever laugh again?

Below The Bridge

Sensitive greens
Tell of lily pads
In still waters
Below a timeless bridge.

Visits to Japan
Made themselves apparent;
And paint made them
Always.
Their just-because
Gives the viewer pause.

The painting's twin is, too, on display
And may some day
Bring its own
Satisfaction.

Fugi, Miles Away

Large, large foreground, wagon, wagon wheels on flat surface—
Contrasting—
Diminutive Fugi.
Far away Fugi.
One dimensional perspective.
Pure primaries dominate.
Tiny Fugi
Focused
In a wave-curl.
Real distance for the mind
N/A.
A closer Fugi
Would lose its mystery;
While Fugi miles away
Anticipates wonder.

Cutoffs

Degas' cut-offs anticipate a world beyond the paintings.
Those subjects who walk only partially within the frame
Walk away from all-inclusive dialectic.
Tradition stands contradicted.
Degas was not just different.
Degas made a difference.
Degas made a new flavor of marmalade.
Degas toasted "piece-meal".

The gentleman and his daughters
Play peek-a-boo
And come bearing Degas' cut-offs.
Will't please you look at them?

Framed In Oil

Many scenes are tamed by outline -
From flower pots to majestic mountains,
Subdued, perhaps, or flowing fountains.
And wood and gold make frames fine.
Deer preserved in paint will feed forever.
Gamecocks on a barn door will bleed apace.
Galloping wild horses will speed in place.
And space, in squares, will infinity sever.

Art's the thing to capture bird on wing.
Brush strokes work to fool the eye
Into accepting a painted blue sky
And atmosphere that speaks of spring.

Devils Tower, Mt. Fugi, Holy Mount,
Glacier Lake,
Glaciers,
Rolling wave,
Painted Desert, redwoods, painters save,
And more than there is time to count.

Mastodonic And Miniature

Forty feet high in rusted steel
A giant to the city's building for preservation,
And, on the table within the inner space, a twelve inch mini,
Stand in contrast.
Ant-like visitors feel toward lofty observation
Of angles, circles, lost-in-space,
And what of all within their sight will last.

Sculpt This

Huge, magnified unto glorious!
A mountain revisited, with faces
Four.
Presidents.
Always taken for granite.
Emerging, none bore glum expressions.
Only what was remembered of their stature
In a nation undivided.

A lady-like figure draped in folds,
Realistic beyond belief,
Un-aging,
Stirring even forbidden feelings.

Giant distortions carved in stone!
On an island? Two islands!
God-like—Stone Henged—a natural face on a mountain, Hawthorne.
Retro-cliff's petrogliphs.
Statuary: Ordered by great leaders, of themselves. Generals.
The youthful King David, nudely viewed and dormantly endowed.
Waxed, having waxed and waned.
Busted to tables and shelves.
Relegated to cardboard cutouts, alabaster.
Distortions due to mind warps, due to linear appeal.
Enormity glorified, background helping.
Arch-i-sculpture buildings as art—
Enriching landscapes.
The spreading of grand drapes—
Sticking together Nature's parts—
Mystified by Cristo, fried—
From the canyon to the city park.
Summation leaves much to be discussed.

Quicker Than The Eye

It began with flickers of quick moves.
Celluloid captured ghostly images.
Herky met Jerky, gobbling actors by the reel,
With subtitles.
Quicker than the eye, stationary-in-motion,
Dispelled the notion, "What is, is not, what 'what is' appears.
Imprinting the film, making sound impressions,
Piano going bye-bye,
35 mm,
Selling mmmm mmmm's over the counter,
Glorious color demanding makeup,
The art of animation brought to greater fruition,
Going digital—
What next, pocket movies?

Color Fling

Jackson Pollack told a fish story
About flinging paint at canvas,
A whale of a tale that dribbled into visions of Rorschach
Led color by the ring finger in excitement.
It, the story, superseded distorted reality
That superseded art that imitated life, nature, reality.

Color fling brought jubilation
From age to age to Pollack to "who am I ?"
To the middle of the deep blue sea.

Patterning

Many stitches in time produce quilts.
A flower promenades and never wilts.
Checkers anyone?
Everyone having fun?
Knick knack boxes overflow.
First prize, in the eyes, is an afterglow.
Though, "just because"
Overcomes beginner's flaws
And justifies what quilters know—
They can quilt away a winter's snow.
They can bring a touch of spring.
They can be material witnesses to art.

Arc Attempts

De Triumph, Texture, Arches with bass relief,
Façade holders for community pillars
Upholding law, etc.
Architecture arc attempts for the ages
Foreshadow new arts of stone.

Potter Clay Play

To throw a pot takes a wheel.
Hands are best for shaping feel.
Bake a pattern in the clay.
Give in to potter clay play.

Notes To The World

Classics, Jazz, Classic Jazz, harmonics, tonal phonics,
Popular, pop, loud-soft,
Bass-a-tutional, sopranoistic, tenorisms, altometrical,
Peace in pastoral, war in marches, bad rap, musical crap, loftiness strung
on harpiness,
hymnatistic thunder and tears, pianoisimo, piano-lumber-loud, brass-a-
dash
scaling, string fingering unto sing-a-linging—
Written with condimental contrapuntal provisional perfection.

On The Walls

Browning's "last duchess"
Stood ever fixed on a stair wall.
And his duke chose never to stoop.
Many Piccassos, Matisses, other moderns
Are ever chosen as a group
 To grace other halls with nudes and ferns,
Rotating to other walls by turns.
Displays have walls assigned
From which to engage the fertile mind
Ever seeking a new find.
The old is stored for showing
On walls desolate of inspection for long hours
Tolled to excess by clock towers.
The line's the thing in which to catch a museum wing
With wall space to capture the portrait of a king,
The face of horror, a soup can, a tapestry from antiquity,
Flowers in sunlight, birds in flight,
The damned from the dens of iniquity,
Streets light and dark,
Drawings by Lewis and Clark—
Always variety.

✖✖✖
OF ORDINARY PEOPLE

Ordinary People

Whitman heard the ordinary people singing.
Sandburg wrote of their pitfalls and catcalls,
Their carryin's on,
Their testament to surprise,
And their continued queries about coming and going.
Balladeers speak of celebrations and feats of hallelujahs and tears of the extraordinarily ordinary people.
Their variety is astounding.
Their passion, responding with confusion,
Speaks of denial and inclusion, of doubt and hurt and indecisive reaction, and small satisfaction.
They, the storied, work, cry, marry, bury, sing, pray, justify, sympathize and endure
generation unto generation with absolution and veneration, and customize their living in story.
 They carry the seeds of glory on their long treks, through abstinence and sex and transfiguration in the face of change.
He who is not ordinary finds it lonely at the top, a place where it is impossible to stop to chat, to charm, and to fight against a long night of evil.
The plains and the hills are alive with ordinary people, succumbing to the piper of nothing resoundingly particular.

Come Gentle People

Come, gentle people, you can relax.
It's a good time of day to play sax,
Stay inside and read the funnies,
Pet the cats and dogs and bunnies.
Come, to the window, see quiet snow fall.
Take a brisk walk up and down the hall.
Get out the paints and splash color,
The brighter the better--never the duller.
Come, gentle people, it's winter, you know.
All the good moisture will make things grow.
Get out the tablet; start planning a garden.
Keep planning and planning. Resolve will harden.
One day the springtime will blow in with warmness.
You'll be grateful for the down time, now harmless.
Come, gentle people, nap through a woe day.
You can always lay low on a snow day.

Perishables

People give rise to their own importance.
And, significantly, not perishing tops their list.
Needed are an ark and a covenant
That satisfy a desire to exist.

All who live are perishable.
Like the grass they have only a while alive on Earth.
Like instruments they play little melodies.
Like voices they sing.
Like flowers they fade into shade and the shadow of no breath.
Then they are gone.
Yet they look from eyes of new life......
On and on and on.

Ghosts Of Transition

No-names. But uncontrollable burning.
Adventure, maybe.
But mostly unconquered need
To get some of the golden gravy,
To escape, to stake a claim,
To lasso a western dream.

The failures of a quest to equal Tabor
Put down roots in Colorado,
Played imaginary flutes conjuring
Lawman and desperado—legends.
Miners from Wales imagined daylight.
Civilized Chinese, scorned,
Labored in the transition that brought the railroad,
Through the territory, westward.

Out of Carolina, out of eastern U.S.A.,
Out of St. Louis, out of clouded judgment,
Out of a crazy quilt of un-reason,
Out of hope—but always into newness,
Always the ghosts becoming the novices, the dreamers, the schemers,
the business man, the entrepreneurs, the lady of ladies, the haphazard and
Unidentified puzzle pieces.
Mountains were tunneled. Ore trains came and went.

Denver gathered all who would dance in transition,
Jockey for position,
Become hub to the ghosts and their ghosts, to the changing.
Denver and territory ballooning outward
race back to ghosts of transition giving territory to communities
identifying
rainbow colors in separation.

Ghosts of the sluice, ghosts of the gamblers, ghosts of the traders—
mountaineers.
Ghosts corporeal—ghosts in turn.
Ghosts of buggy horses, dray horses, plow horses
Gone into transition, into metal and glass powered by explosions.

Big river. Decisive politics of water people
Ghost away into repetition
As dams become fences for farmers.
Progeny beat the war drums in time of need.
The moneyed look on with greed.
Ghost water, held up high, transitions through time into fullness, and slim
pickings.
Magenta, a clown figure representing ghost women, wives in hardscrabble
Talking to a modern man, one of dog walks and fly fishing,
Himself in transition from a ghost in fishing past—
A long way from the ghosts of mountains newly formed.

A long succession of old gentry transitioning through notoriety,
wealthifying,
(Polo in Colorado?) Antiques, Greek and otherwise.
Great grandpa worked his ass off
And children's children became collectors,
Purveyors of art and community uplift, society page photos and captions.

Ghost towns speak of ghosts of beginnings, of through-boom-to-bust and
tumbling
into dust.
Old wood decaying testifies to old life and lust and thirst for success, and
failed economy
and move on.

Statehood the big leap—
Colorado of the Union—
Union busting. Ghost victims—
Corporate posturing—
Nickel and dime workers—
News ghosted from then to now in transition, then and now-a-days.
Ghosts of tomorrow read reports and pray.

Birth Of Promise

Newness of life, instant success,
Nakedness unadorned at egress,
Perfection held high
To produce a cry
To begin a new life of stress.
Cute unto learning and praise,
Yet constrained in some ways.
Perfection is denied to conforming's ride
 That constructs a harrowing maze.

The promise comes certified.

Dreams Infinite

Skyward. And dreams defy gravity.
Just getting by implies gravity
Of situation
That seems permanent
And for the duration.
Yet, dreams infinite, beyond limitation,
Dressed as possibilities,
Adhere always.

They are their own reality.

Nonogenerational

Getting there is half the fun.
The other half is an end run
Around accidental demise
Before ninety.
Now the race to a hundred,
Infinity and all,
Medicated all to hell and all,
Indoctrinated with crap
About too old and all.
A hundred comes in careful baby steps,
Or on wheels.

Century Transitional

A big smile and remembrance is for now.
A century from the cradle
And yet no grave,
But somehow there is comfort in its wave.
Its beaconing is more than reckoning.
It can literally fill a void.

Disarray disappears beyond a hundred years
Along with at least a hundred fears.

A wink and the beyond thing is.

Spirals Interrupted

Old roses are clipped;
And new ones are formed.
They are hardened
As they are stormed.
They can go crazy as they grow wild,
Or conform in beauty
As a well trained child,
Until death.
Both have spirals interrupted.

Spiral-Ed Wunderbar

A small beginning, insignificant,
 Pretty much is yeasted toward magnificent
As a life snowballs
And questioning becomes affirmation.
And yes, and yes, and yes
Become an over-all appellation
For world without end.
Let the glorious ascend
The spiral-ed Wunderbar.

As If By Magic

The poet won't show it, but wants to put words together in a
way that will exactly say
Who is who and what is whether, as if by magic.
The music schooler can play the fooler, putting on the face of a scholar,
But wants the magic in understanding to determine a Mendelssohn or a
Mahler.
The artist will try to use an eye to conjure up a
piece of per diem that creates a vision by his precision
And works magically with a medium.
An actor will hide with some pride behind a mask
to deceive. The illusion factor will hide inside
A love of make-believe.
What's not exposed when it's not supposed
That magic is not explainable,
Is, what is not, is carried on the back of what is sustainable.
Comic or tragic, it's all done as if by magic.

Ennui, Old Witch

Ennui, old witch, move over. As long as I'm in my mind a rover,
You cannot occupy a royal chair or have me pulling my hair.
Kept without the gate, you can starve for all I care!
I would sing at Heaven's gate, having remanded my soul there
to wait,
Long before your toil and trouble could invade my mental state
And lay me in state with blasé.

Tasting Accents

Place any mind in the center,
Accents revolve around it.
English as she is spoke, German, Swedish,
 Pole to Pole, grammar split,
 Knock-about Yankee carpenter,
Anything that can be made to fit.
Taste test reveals sweet, sour, salty, faulty,
 But never bitter within getting-to-know-you.
Open says-a-me, Mandarin mind,
Cockney, Welsh, French, Spanish, Tutu—
Receive them as you would any pleasurable find.
 Wear them as you would any comfortable old shoe.

Pass-Around Table

Grace—Amen
Pass the Virginia ham, Virginia,
Sweet potatoes if you please.
Cheat a little.
 Make a space.
Let Charley sit down.
Pass the relish dish and the Roquefort cheese.
The dining table by extension is double clothed,
Which hides a make-shift invention of odd pieces.
Chairs at roundup time greatly vary.
 Some unfold for nephews and nieces.
Variations on a theme
Can have Cold Duck with roast duck,
Cabernet with potluck
White and blush with chicken.
After dinner heavy can still hold rose.

Stranded In Utopia

A comfort level of sameness
Installed itself in a life.
The blips were minor.
The days to days were predictable.
Auto-pilot threaded the life
Through the narrow passage
 Between Heaven and Hell..
The youth conformed innocuously.
Then, manhood unsettled him,
Still stranded in Utopia.

So Unfinished

Girl, bird-like, has bones showing at sharp angles—
Shoulders, hips, elbows, knees.
Girl grew up learning how to please.
Delicate, precise, are her movements.
Her bow is slight and unobtrusive.
Yet she has strength in her rejection of some wishes.
She draws a line.
She has drawn herself incomplete by design.
All curry her favor;
She is much in demand.
Gratitude?
Not even for the greatest gratuity.
All or any is only if she chooses.
All is a game, and she never loses.

All Is Calm

Well dressed gentleman waits patiently.
He is shy, introspective.
He has a need
Above and beyond what he has done to succeed.
He is aware she has no clock.
In a moment, after meditation,
She will appear,
Front open
Nakedly appealing,
She will serve him tea and disappear.

He has disrobed and entered a sauna.
She stands statue-like, waiting.
She is motionless and ornamental
Within his sightline.
He rises from the pool to air dry.
He moves slowly to the massage table and lies down.
Her measured movements have mirrored his—
She carries massage oils.
She waits through his napping.
Oils are applied.
She expertly touches Erogenous,
Then massages limp into ecstasy.

Transient State Of Love

Arduous in long moments of pastime,
Two embrace.
Nerves process information;
And an act of love is consummated.
She, toy by design, enjoys his inflation.
And she mouths words to prolong fulfillment,
Her face a mask.
He must not know he is her best customer,
Would get whatever he would ask.

What is a time but transitory and move on?
Yet some can be prolonged for pleasure.
No clock would toll one's life,
Or quiet endurance,
Or a brief time of leisure.

His emotion spilled into relaxing,
Conditions her release.
And in quiet elation,
For him her time does cease.

The patient one rises without words
And departs.
She sleeps, bemused.

Lunch Pail Gangs

Rail Yards chuffing sounds,
Scrung and scree and long, shivering scrum,
Song of engine-at- work in the freight yards.
 Forth and reverse and new connects
Resurrects a new freight train.
Night work goes on with lanterns, headlamps, and smoke from coal fires.
 Rail cars, getting sidetracked by the numbers,
Make up runs—east, west, north, south—
 Ready to cross the river, follow the river, wend over miles to Wendover,
Rockford,
Scranton, as far as Pasadena.
 And, a gang makes the show go.
Stripes, overalls, tall cap with stripes—
Engineer stands tall in a tall cab.
His bucket is stashed for noon.
His mind is on his work.
He is an expert driver.
He reads signals and freight is collected.
He will take a run tomorrow down to Hampton.
Passengers on the grade will wait.
He of the deft leap pulls a switch and rails change.
And the concert begins.
He wields the baton.
Roundhouse machinist with massive wrenches and oil cans and a lifetime of
experience
repairs, retools, restores, returns giants of iron and steel to workloads.
Handcars—handles pumped in rhythm make them go,
As gandydancers check for flaws.
Rail alignment is crucial
As seated passengers ride.

"Your best part of the day is what?"
"Lunch."
Early to rise.

Chow down with eggs and fries.
Hit the track
With motion transfer and clickity clack.
We dance a fierce fantastic.
Pry bar in hand, our time is elastic.
"What's in your bucket?" "Pie. What's in yours?"
"Rhubarb again. Guess I'll chuck it."
 Home to line shack, pain felt. Pop the tops on several Grainbelt
Or several Coors.
Pale, vested ticket agent sits and waits for the crowded-station times.
 He will be on the hurry-go soon enough:
Check luggage, hurry-go
Ticket transfers, hurry-go
Answer questions, hurry-go
Between bites, hurry-go
To stave off hunger from hurry-go.
Multi-tasking agent has a rhythm
That gets him through the day.
Train crews get used to power lunches.

Steel Mill

Accident and hospital and no lunch; lunch goes on.
Hooks and cranes and crane operators
And molten metal shapers and dippers,
 Rivet makers.
Body parts to the auto makers.
 Rails to the railroads.
Beams to the builders of buildings.
Factory whistle to big eaters, "chow time!"
Then work goes on into the night
With muscle, main and might.

Docks

And freight handlers everywhere.
Pass the mustard and cut the cheese and have a fight.
And work goes on, loading and unloading:
Warehouse—union
Airplane docking area—union
Shipyards, union
Major trucking-union
"Bring the forks over here!"
"Load by the numbers
"Get the lead out of your ass!"
The hour is at hand to open the buckets.
Hard hats have nasty stories with their lunch-
Nantucket comes to mind.

Way up high

A skywalker guides a girder.
A clear day and he can see forever.
Sure-footed, balanced, ready to eat. But, first, the girder homed.
(Lunch can be shared with the birds.) Signals are well practiced
and precise.
Cinched and tied—that's it.

"God damn! Look at the size of that banana!"
"My package has a big banana. Ripe, too."
"When was the last time it got peeled?"
"See that down on 53rd street? Skirt up to her ass? Last night"
"Her?"
"Name's Mary Jean. Works over at Compton Press."
"She got a sister?"

Cones

Watch the red cones. Guide the traffic
Around the stripper shooter
Filling trucks with old and worn
One day;
Around the lane layer another;
Around pothole fillers
Wielding shovels and rakes
Down the road and around the corner.

The gathering of the faithful at noon
In a spot of shade
A row of trees has made, though little,
Lunch pails open.

One can hear misbegotten English.
Or Latino lingo—
Loud talking, boisterous.
(Road gangs)
I got chili peppers. Want one?
"Too goddamn hot for me!"
"Good for what ails you."

Brown

What can brown sack do?
It can fit a drawer or a fridge;
It can be a filling bridge until dinner.
It can be the lunch pail for the office crew.
Gangs are always packin'.

A Town Talks

Steepled Past:

An all white column, with its bells, pointing to the yesteryears,
Stands upon St. Andrew's stone and speaks of gloried past.
"I have weathered well since Wier's beginning, its hopes and fears, its
sadness and its tears, its works in war with eyes downcast, and its
triumphant new invention of happiness times at last.

"I stand at the southern end of Water Street and call Episcopalians to
enter a house of God for worship in spite of hurt and pride.
I join the peels from other steeples to summon all theist-o-palians to
prayer, to work, to sing in adoration, to honor those who died, to be
among the throng of those 'do-God's-will-without-failians'."

A Quarry's Issue:

My stone, cut and patterned, is displayed all over town on
buildings, fronting streets in parallels, with great renown.
 I am well marbled for a majestic presentation to the world;
But my town is twice blessed in living in a way that's pearled.

Shoebox Clientele:

"I am trailer size, a counter and eight stools that fit many sized stoolers.
They are the counter culture in overalls, suits and whatever, not measured
by rulers.
 I encounter whoever partakes of greasy fast foods, donuts, coffee, soft
drinks, at various times and in various spaces, with or without cubed ice
that clinks.
 I am The Shoebox set on a downgrade with a well stocked larder and a
lard filled owner;
and I'm not very far removed from a car-filled and busy and bustling
street corner."

Edifices Rock:

"We are singing with great stone faces of fashion wear, of jewelry, hotel
clientele, of fine furniture.
We are window-wide with grand displays and are lighted well in
evenings.
Up we go with offices. Up we go with shiny windows. Up we go beyond
our flagpoles,
our flagstaffs, our flags.
We hold secrets in our cornerstones. We stand mute beside the passers-
by with flighty
goals, beside the slow of heart who lags, beside the shopping one with
bags.
We are grand and permanent containers that hold prosperity. We are
strong and mighty.
We are downtown, images pointing to the past, the present, and beyond.
We 'siggle' each other with codes in our heads from winter wind and
snow, gossiping of
juicy things we know. We are imbued with life."

Town Crier:

"Whatever cries out to be read, fills my pages; and I decide that
many times.

 What, when, why, where, who and how of the here and now is
inked, at least until tomorrow
and its updates.
I am paper, cut and pasted. I hold many bits to be tasted. None of my
space is wasted.
I am the Town Crier, and, often a political crucifier because of a belief by
my editor-in-chief
who despises a liar.

I put the screws to the bad news about those who win and
those who lose.

I don't mind being 'pressed' into service."

Old with Rain:

"A trestled bridge, I go way back to the beginning of the railroad through
the outskirts of
Weir, spurred on by payloads.
May loads continue to cross my tracks with furious clickity-clacks.
For more than a hundred years, aged in rain, I have witnessed endless
strings of railcars
come, pass, and go.
 Much I know of the commerce of the town.
Much I know of what makes the economy transition to up and to down.
I have bridged many ups and downs. I enjoy the 'whistle-throughs'."

Cracks and Weeds:

"Old Weir crumbles. I have witnessed my shine's disappearance.
 I was a proud walkway around every block of homes.
Now I'm humble as I crumble and walkers stumble.
I have been wind dusted and infested with weeds,
Cracks that feed weed seed, weeds that multiply."

I am Modern. I am Steel and Glass:

"I have spread in a new age by the acre.
If Madam Progress is asleep, I wake her.
I comprise the modern buildings. I am steel and glass.
I rise as high rise buildings above flower beds and grass.
I tower high and look out upon the new park,
The golf course, the super highway.
I do things my way."

Garden Pleasures

Memorial Stone:

Coming to a stone garden alone, one of the living takes a turn at care giving
In remembrance of the sincerely departed.
That one is concerned that fresh flowers be placed upon the graveyard plot
To honor what in life had been started.
She, the one of the living, thought she saw his face upon the granite gravestone.
Apparition like, it appeared and left again.
Momentarily, other stones had other faces with attractive traces of life on earth,
Playing games, weird, of 'remember when?'

Strings in a Veggie Plot:

A yarn can be stretched so far; and yet it can be used as string in a veggie plot.
 How about a skyscraper beginning for a Jacked beanstalk up to giant land?
How about if violins played soothing music as stimulation in a high garden spot?
 What if roofers had to wait for carrots, cucumbers, radishes, and lettuce to ripen?
 Let's just say there are issues involved with riding an elevator to water a lot.

Fleur de Whatever:

It is fashionable in France to be concerned about what in a vineyard
creates distinction.
Noteworthy is the lengths to which French go in preserving bouquet of
modified fruit.
There is a passion in the fashion of representing red, white, or other as
aged to perfection.

And the contents are guaranteed to contain nothing impure, at least subject
to detection.
"Essence of lily" could bring a great auction price if one were to engage in
such a pursuit.

Heather Holiday:

Gang the hither. Look out upon the land that is good for nothing else.
Wonder whether God planned something else and changed his mind.
Or, a cover of color all along, may have been what God had designed;
And nothing mattered in the grand scheme of things for Scots
As long as they deemed themselves fortunate not to be color blind.
When heather blooms grandly, in great expanse, in unending undulation,
Take a train to nowhere in particular on a particular holiday sometime.
Take a gander. See if the sea of flowering, flowing, fills you with sublime
Anticipation for the rest of the northern Isle's immensely glowing
grandeur.
Attempt to describe what you have seen in appropriately glowing rhyme.

Upon The Rooftop:

Urbanese do what they please with gardens upon the rooftops
Far above the walks and streets that mix modern cars with hoof clops.
In evening dress one can confess he or she has hired a gardener
Who can, depending on the right conditioner, be a softener or a hardener.
Tropical trees in tubs for easy removal sway in accents of faux scenery.
A mini park transcends all bustling activity with silent, beautiful greenery.
A rooftop door has climbers that dress up its effrontery, being plain in egress.
Pipes are hidden; and surrounding walls can be painted as waterfalls, no less.
Are wildlife creatures kept in cages as all of the caretakers earn their wages?
Perhaps they peek in furtive manner while readers read then turn the pages.
It's safe to say that Santa and his reindeer, when green is removed, could land
To take a breather, and sit upon a park bench, and smoke the pipe bowl grand.

God's Billion:

A billion light years away from an explosion and a new Eden untarnished by Earth
Furnished a new beginning for a new beginning to a new beginning and a new birth.
Coming to the garden alone, a man of great distinction, refined, and of great worth
Babbled incomprehensively over what to take seriously and what to take as mirth.

Until a soul mate appeared and laughed and everything went downhill from hith girth

To hith exthaggerated ability to be Godth's buddy and confidant, and hith ability to curth.

Alive with Sound: BZZZZZZZZZZZZZ!

Down By The Levi

The old lady got her feet wet up to her eyebrows.
And her tens of thousands fled for their very lives.
Much disquiet discussed the wherefores and the whys and hows
To the tune of row, row, row your boat toward one who survives.

From destructive hurricane's deadly path
Came a dirty, toxic bath,
A witch's cauldron—
A devil's brew—
And its consequence of wrath.

Old Lady, have you not yet drowned? Will there
yet be a second time
around? Will your bustle be a thing to admire?
New fame perhaps you
will acquire.

You were fabled for jazz—
Hirt, Fountain, bands with pzazz.
All have been tabled for a duration While gods
have been appeased
With oblation.

Strike up a parade for the Old Lady's passing.
Make way for the thousands in the New Lady, amassing.

Sleeping Futures

Sleepy time—
And mommas do rock them
In their cradles.
Out of Mexican they hear Mexican.
Out of Latino they hear Latino—
Out of a great culture
That they will carry to new cradles.
Sleeping beauties, sleeping cuties,
They are sleeping futures.
Hearing the call of America singing,
Hearing a heritage joining the song,
Will they stay beautiful?

And So, Freedom

When alabaster cities gleam
And mountain tops are beautiful,
They reflect the buried shame
Of a tearful enslavement.
1864, Lincoln logged in a proclamation.
Its purpose was to name a freedom
That fulfilled a potent dream
And preoccupation with dutiful,
Putting an end to a cruel game—
Entombed for all time with engraving.
Documentation—
And so, freedom

The Future By The Acre

A world's fair in a fair world
Announced the wonders of the future.
Exciting scriptwriting gripped the patrons where
They stood in awe.
An infant strolled where tales were told.
Not even a future by the acre could wake her.
Motor cars driven half way to the stars
Might overtake her.
OK, Sara?

Cycle Through Life

Cycle through life.
Peddle slowly, peddle slowly.
Stay focused on being unfocused.
Stop to feel the soul.

Hurry not nor tarry too long
With viewing the familiar.
Peddle slowly, peddle slowly,
Tasting the wine of each day.

Hand in hand, cycle
With someone you love.
Peddle slowly, peddle slowly,
To travel in style.

Peddle slowly, peddle slowly
To cover each mile.
Peddle slowly, peddle slowly,
To enjoy a grand view.

For A Quiet Time

Imagine a tree in a meadow
With a stream drifting by.
Let lines from a song fill your dreaming.
Give not a thought for when you'll die.
In pictures of past loves and the present
Pasture-eyes everything that is pleasant.
True comforts of home supply.
Maybe with firelight gleaming
You'll never have to ask, why".

That Final Step

Ever look for a timeless afternoon
When the forgotten clock disappears?
And much from seamless application
Of skills dispels your fears?
Ever pass up an opportunity
To enter eternity for a while,
In need of caring for tomorrow
While feeding a "crocodile"?
Take that final step across the threshold
Run those unseen minutes off a mile.
Put yourself in a place of timelessness
To be nowhere for a while.

Everywhere Goodbye

No new destination awaits the perfect drummer.
His assignments had been global,
Fall, winter, spring, and summer.
Prague in winter was a bitch,
Though his time there went without a hitch.
He had paved the way for presidents.
He had glad-handed many residents.
His pasted smile and energy
Created perfect synergy
For perfect get-togethers,
For high level talks--
Despite the weather,
Despite how "the wind blew",
Despite the caustic commentary
By members of the press crew.
Mr. Ambassador took to sunny climes with pleasure
And whiled away more time than was good
In sumptuous visitation to pleasure places
And many endearing spaces.
Yet, he was formidable and respected.
His programs, when dissected,
Revealed the super prowess of his tenures,
For many more than ten years.
He could retire
And fulfill his heart's desire
For happy, unrestricted, wanderings.

Retreats For Comfort

That place with window bars and gated entry....
That park for pedestrians with a remembrance tree....
That easy chair with an open book upon an end table
Presenting to the reader some grand fable....
That workroom with scatter everywhere....
That peaceful nook or cranny without window glare....
That train or trolley ride to the library
To bring home Bacon or Trollope, or Mc Clary....
That animal farm with menagerie called zoo....
That ride in the country to observe something new....
That retreat for comfort never hurt anyone.
It's good, once in a while to become undone.

And Tomorrow Is Ok

A tomorrow over the rainbow is ok,
Ever pointing to a Sunday in the park,
Distilling whatever makes a mark
That signifies a mix of pleasure
Taken in the treasure of a new day.
And destruction bred out of Man,
No recollection of how or when.
A day of salvation everywhere then
Became a covering flag of will
In order to fulfill a master plan.
All-a-man left and do-se-do.
Bow and curtsy all around.
No distress can be found
To interrupt a grand display
Of where a future day can go.
No worries in that tomorrow.

The Moment Of Yes

"Where ya goin, Pilgrim?"
"Out there beyond the pale
Where monsters of the deep dwell."

Story—belief—yes

"How do ya dare, Pilgrim?"
"It's in God's hands. I must go and see."

Many moments of the story of "yes" occupy the pages of time—
Even into that great ocean of nothing called space.

Old Friend

I see you not often;
But, I send good wishes your way.
 You will have to pardon my Christian friend.
He looks at all you survey and sees God,
The captain of his captured soul.
He brings baggage on his journey.
Treat him with kindness.
The Ark is his to guard.

A Sense Of Tranquility

Forget the reasoning
Behind all the dance steps
Toward self knowledge.
Forget the unconquered.
Forget the meaningless toil.
Don't try to escape the pleasant.
Dust for the finger prints of peace.
Check for all means of escape
 To a sense of tranquility.

Teaching Christmas

A cat taught me Christmas
When I looked with wide eyes at opulence,
Thinking Christmas was what this was.
It lay nearby,
Wanting nothing but my company.
Then it slept, and I…..
Both contented just to be.

A Cup of Kindness

Story of a desert walker and a cup of water,
Just a halfway marker to an oasis,
A small hollow in sand holding two handfuls.
Was the walker guided to the water?
Or, was discovery accidental?
Did the walker need the water?
Did the walker take the water?
Or, did the walker leave the water for another walker?
Would the water be restored?
Would the water be ignored?
Would the walker be assured the wonder water would suffice?
Would the walker believe in Someone's being nice?

The Always Sled

A Christmas sled,
A downhill ride
On snow thick and cold.
Winter trees are spare.
Wraps warm the body,
But not the cheeks.
And glide with smooth lasts a lifetime.

Runners still carry a child.
Stillness haunts memory.
A sit-back picture
Brings distance closer.
Details unfold.

Overalls, tennis shoes,
Coat slightly outgrown,
Clothe a belly flopper—
Legs bent upward.
A background of white
Moves with speed.

Swimming In Salad

The plowman wends his weary ways,
Eating main course salad days.
Grueling, swimming upstream against the tide,
The plowman remains numb to an easier ride,
Knows nothing of uplifting pride.
Tortured time does not the flower give
To accent a life he must live.
Swimming in salad sour,
He wends hour after hour.
And he dies to the chime
From a clock's foreboding tower.

Good To Go

Fast good, put up ahead of time,
In mood, in attitude, as soul food,
Will not spoil. It is good—to go,
At the ready.

It does not toil or spin,
Nor know what deserving means.
It is distinguished by
What is not relinquished with "why".

A Game Of Check Yours

"Who are you today?"
Talks of curls on foreheads,
Of pearl and wisdom other days.
Balking at unseemly forays,
Or going on them,
Answers the question
Posed under autosuggestion—
"Who are you today?"

Where Smiles Are

Way out where the doggies bawl
And the rooky gets snookered by the old hand,
Where the smiles are.
Where the Wabash Cannonball
Brings a visitor by rail car,
Smiles are.
Cherry blossom time, through the arches,
Jack-o-lope country,
Mountain's majesty.
Sprawling western city of dreams,
Morning coffee and funnies,
Serendipitous humor ala conversation.
(Pick your poison.)
Where smiles are, be.

Westerin'

ONE:

There was a time of wood buildings
Of coal stoves and flues and stovepipe
Of General Stores and trappings
Before their appearance, were campfires and bedrolls and cattle
Sheepherding and feuds
Open range, then fences
Raids and retribution
Mines—gold and silver—
(The use of periods suggests separation)
A milieu, a mix, a slowly changing meld
A shift
A price of doing business
Oil—shale—
A lot of country living
Rugged individuals, women and men
Mountains, prairies, desserts
Living off the land, on the land
Provincial parochial
Learned—the homegrown and the funneled in
Farmland and homesteads
 Bulls, mules, range horses
Civilization in transition, civilized

Over the mountain to paradise
Dust and dirt and starvation
Left for a land of plenty
Invaded out of desperation
Out of dreams obsessed

Story:

Giants roamed the earth
Giants in the earth
Giants unearthed
Dinosaurs died; their skeletons were revealed as history
The long road to Typarary
Came out of a long-a-go past
Much has been made of dinosaurs
Much has been made of floods
Man's beginning has been queried
Ant-like, spread over millennia
Came, finally, west and west of west
Inland albatross were legion
Hard luck stories abounded
They were not confined to any region
Their clarion calls were widely sounded

The continent had only sea coast and mountains and vast wilderness
But not for long would they not be apprehended

Story:

Rivers, tributaries, gulfs, oceans
Piano in the mud, lifted, rescued, symbol of the genius that is in the arts

Story:

A mountain man killed a bear when he was only three
Jumpin' Judas! Could that really be?

Story:

Gold, Rush, Dig,
Rich and bust, opulence and harshness, mad dash and mad lady of the
Matchless Mine
Silver lining—rock and hair,
Mines played out, story played out

TWO:

Same old:
For the beauty of the earth
For purple mountains' majesty
For waviness of grain
Forever high flying flag
For comfort zones and enthusiasm
For "We are the cat's pajamas"
For booziness and churchliness toward unfettered freedom
And, all together now, "We are the bestest"

Contrast:

War powers acts and other shameful ones
Sandberg's observations balled up in a fist
Shaking in despair over truth hidden
That, if revealed, would make sailors blush
Conquistadores, Spanish for "gotcha!"
Started something that spread,
Exploration, conquest, open a can of worms
Two hundred years---then westering
West of north, whatever floats your boat
Lewis, Clark, whatever notes they wrote,
From Washington to Washington
With whatever boats to tote
Ah! Lake-full waters, Indian lands
Zebulon Pike got a peek at a peak,
A Rocky Mountain Gee-whiz!
Imagine getting to the top of Pikes Peak
One step at a time
Over hundreds of decades nooks and crannies were filling
Tiny civilizations came and went or were perpetuated
Distances measured in days or weeks
Was there a Westerin' star
To guide the westerin' man?
Wagoning and walking at a measured pace,
Potential populace helter-skeltered across the landscape
Amid continued soreness and sore afraid and sorrow and perseverance
Children of God kept coming, kept being born
Mythical creatures played out their little dramas,
Segued from one consequence to another

Weather:

Too damned hot, too damned cold, too damned dry, too damned wet

Mountains
 Too damned steep, too damned high
Dust or snow whipped against the face, Mexico to Montana
Milling around the mountains—
The mountains held buried treasure
Saw nuggets turn into chandeliers
Saw rockyites go European
Saw polo come to Denver
Saw mucho grasses feed the cattle that fed the miners,
Their mucho gracias evident in their energy

ESCAPEES:

In hock to lenders, packer-uppers
Changed their names and headed into the sunset,
Rolled with wheeled wagons whited with canvas and crammed for a long
haul
Trained they were for preservation, or not,
Picked they anonymity against their balls and chains
Suffering prairie fatigue, some stopped and stayed
Well stocked and of the spirit,
Persecuted of the Lord
Took patience westward,
Their victims of ills of the flesh
Buried, Bibled, remembered

Billion was an unfathomed number
But thousands endured the roll-ons, the walk-a-thons, afoot or astride
Caught up in A.W.O.L. and a need to disappear,
A lonely tramper left his past behind
IN 1810 he gathered what belongings would sustain him
The trek called avoidance measured the upward miles
He cautioned himself against great expectations
No good could come of extradition
He told himself to shun social contact
He would be a hermit in the legendary mountains
In freedom he measured the byways traveled
By moon and stars and not by miles,
Wandering
In song and story the loner
Became a part of the ongoing legends

TESTIMONY:

Around tables, over drinks,
Mighty figures were extolled, buckskinned, and braveried,
Were outlawed and in-lawed
And exaggerated beyond belief
"Abe could split a log with one blow!"
"Abe walked fifteen miles to return three cents in change."
"Abe walked on water."
"Lincoln's log cabin leaked"
"He had to hollow out log pieces for buckets."
"Lincoln walked a hundred and fifty miles to win a bet."

"Davey Crocket was a crack shot.
He picked off five hundred Frenchies before they fried him."
"Jessie James could stop a train in its tracks.
He'd hypnotize the engineer from a thousand yards."
"Winslow homered his first time at bat, hit sixteen in a row, and painted
the cistern by the chapel on the
corners with fast pitches."
"Little Crow came off the reservation to challenge the champion, a giant
of a man. Little Crow got in
seventeen licks before Big Ugly moved a muscle. Little Crow was the
first to be called "Bantam
Rooster."
"Grandpa Chester won a banjo contest at a hundred and fourteen."
"Grandma shelled peas so fast everyone had to come to dinner early. Her
chicken was in the pan before
it was dead."
"A giant grizzly was another of Paul Bunyan's pets."
Like Jimmy Durante they had "a million of 'um".
School yard fights then school yard mentality
Produced wars
North and South and East of West
"Mine is bigger'n yorn" produced pissin' contests.
Love, hate relationships
Grant and Lee never hugged
They were professionals
California was already fools after gold
The golden spike said,
"Sea to shining sea".

EPILOGUE:

Cumberland and Davey Crocket
Inventions to work the land
Household "things"
Outfitters' dream catchers
Explorers
Trappers
Miners
Ne'r-do-wells
Farmers
Ranchers
Eastern cows
Things of the East
Even things of the Orient
Are leaning ever Westward.

Dawns Anew

The dawn comes up then goes away.
The day is fine—
Until the news that someone died.
The breath attached to family ceased.
And the one bereft has cried.

Wounded is another way of tasting
What is of sour bred
And has the name of (sadly) Sorrow's bread.
But, then, some joy is reached
In many dawns ahead.

When Old Is Fun

The gathering of the seventies and eighties,
They of the old who can laugh,
At the antique humor, the gaff,
Dust off the good rumor, the story,
Hello ha, ha's.
Losing the blahs
With goodness sake! smiles,
Instead of rolling in the aisles,
Sets a fun mood that discards the weighty.

Couples, still going to dinner theater,
Play dress up for the occasion.
They've seen the play several times
And applaud with only gentle persuasion,
Whispering who-done-it in act one
Before they've heard the crimes.
They cheer the young singers;
And they over tip their waiter.

Slim and erect from lots of square dance—
Elegantly attired, smartly, the ageless
Go smoothly and are young at first glance.
They can do sets without error, too.
Their book of life is seemingly page-less.
Couples pass on couples when passing on.
They note time passing only by chance.

Reverence suits them particularly well,
Certainly for life, certainly for beyond,
Certainly for every way they can respond,
And most certainly in making contact with their peers.

They are forever never thinking of losing breath,
Always mindful of their years,
Always within a story they can tell.

When old has laughter, old is fun.
And they all give their lives a good run.

Who Am I Today?

Bastard? Hardly.
Interesting person for tabloid reader? No.
Yet, an ongoing number of hats I wear.
Who am I today?
Man with a hoe one day, man with a rake another.
Man in a chef's apron attempting a cake.
Man of leisure one day, too lazy to move.
Of a Sunday morning with newspaper and church,
Afternoons with ballgames on T.V.
Wait for the car to be serviced.
Careful shopper one day a week.
But, who am I today?
A doer of laundry.

I Knew A Mary

(Mary Miners: In memoriam)

I did know a Lady,
Grand in stature,
Silver-haired at thirty nine.
A husky-voiced librarian,
Mary talked and talked and talked.
She lived a walk away
From where she worked.
So, she walked.

Oh! Throaty timeless laugh—
Unleashed in wall-building jeans!
Cancer from smoking
Finally took you away.

(She had married a Gene
Who drove a truck.
Two weeks, and he, too, was gone.)

I Could Wish

"If wishes were horses, beggars would ride"
Goes an old something bromide.
Yet I could wish for a time and place
More in tune with the joys
Of the human race,
Like unto another's joys
Assumed with unassuming grace:
That one's countenance that continually smiles,
Someone's sardonic wit that forever beguiles.
I could ask for a better card: I could wish.
But I am afraid that fortune
Would tell me to go fish.

Transposed

She of the broad persuasion and broad disposition
Defined her life in terms of a broad's profession.
She of the soft curls and soft curves and soft skin
Spoke softly without some conscious thought of sin.
Parading her traffic in evening's chill, immodest dress,
Blondie, in her forties, coughed on a regular basis
As her cigarette smoking gave her eights and aces.

There was no quit in her as she smoked and trolled
And smiled sincerely toward lookers who were bold.
She hooked some johns in random, unordered, selection.
Though she knew how to treat them and take direction.

Her life now was not all she had ever possessed.
Her life had been encased in loving family, blessed.
She had given herself as a bride of Christ then reneged;
Then in guilt and disharmony forgiveness begged.

She had married. She had given birth. She was content.
She certainly believed her children had been heaven-sent.
She looked forward to her unhurried days of peaceful quiet.
She even looked forward to lettuce in her slimming diet.

Blondie, Jenny McGrath, suddenly took to an ugly path,
As she did a Madame Bovary and walked away in wrath
Brought on by "salt" put into wounds by uncaring others,
Husband, in-laws, children, friends, sisters, brothers.

Transposed in a dream ungodly real, she loudly screamed.
The house came alive; and into her room her family streamed.

Now she was grey; now she was widowed, now mixed up.
But, she was still grandma! Her "love" life was again fixed up.

Both Sides Now

She is gone now.
It was she who took thrifty to heart.
Sayings passed down from long ago
Gave her daughter the lessons to follow.

"A penny saved is a penny earned.
Take bargains to heart,
Be thrifty and save and don't fill the cart.
Only take care of your needs", Mother said.

Recipes came down, passed on through generations.
She learned cooking and passed it on.
Her daughter remembers her pot roast, her casseroles, her pies.
Her daughter remembers the thrift in her eyes,
The look she has given her own daughter.

www.ingramcontent.com/pod-product-compliance
Lightning Source LLC
Chambersburg PA
CBHW030109070426
42448CB00036B/573